GETTING TO KNOW
THE U.S. PRESIDENTS

FRANKLIN
PIERCE

FOURTEENTH PRESIDENT
1853 – 1857

WRITTEN AND ILLUSTRATED BY MIKE VENEZIA

CHILDREN'S PRESS®
A DIVISION OF SCHOLASTIC INC.
NEW YORK   TORONTO   LONDON   AUCKLAND   SYDNEY
MEXICO CITY   NEW DELHI   HONG KONG
DANBURY, CONNECTICUT

Reading Consultant: Nanci R. Vargus, Ed.D., Assistant Professor, School of Education, University of Indianapolis

Historical Consultant: Marc J. Selverstone, Ph.D., Assistant Professor, Miller Center of Public Affairs, University of Virginia

Photographs © 2005: Art Resource, NY/National Portrait Gallery, Smithsonian Institution, Washington, DC, USA: 3, 32; Bowdoin College Archives, Brunswick, Maine: 10; Corbis Images/Bettmann: 24, 30, 31; Dembinsky Photo Assoc./G. Alan Nelson: 27; Library of Congress: 17, 21, 26; New Hampshire Historical Society: 14 (Museum of New Hampshire History/Henry Willard), 19; North Wind Picture Archives: 28; White House Historical Association: 4, 25.

Colorist for illustrations: Dave Ludwig

Library of Congress Cataloging-in-Publication Data

Venezia, Mike.
  Franklin Pierce / written and illustrated by Mike Venezia.
    p. cm. — (Getting to know the U.S. presidents)
  ISBN 0-516-22619-3 (lib. bdg.)   0-516-25485-5 (pbk.)
1. Pierce, Franklin, 1804-1869—Juvenile literature. 2. Presidents—United States-—Biography—Juvenile literature. I. Title.
  E432.V46 2005
  973.6'6'092–dc22

                              2004022571

1 2 3 4 5 6 7 8 9 10 R 14 13 12 11 10 09 08 07 06 05

A portrait of Franklin Pierce by George P.A. Healy (National Portrait Gallery, Smithsonian Institution)

Franklin Pierce was the fourteenth president of the United States. He was born in 1804 in Hillsborough, New Hampshire. Franklin was one of the unhappiest U.S. presidents. He had to deal not only with a country headed for civil war, but also with heartbreaking family tragedies.

Jane Pierce and her son Bennie

Sadly, Franklin's first two sons died as young children. Then, just two months before Franklin became president, he lost his third son, eleven-year-old Bennie. The Pierce family was on a train when it derailed. Franklin and his wife, Jane, were only slightly injured in the wreck, but Bennie was killed. Franklin and Jane Pierce never got over the horrible tragedy.

Franklin Pierce had to use
all of his strength to take on the
difficult job of being president.
It was a terrible time in American history.
The northern and southern states were
splitting apart. They couldn't agree on which

MAP SHOWING THE
UNITED STATES &
TERRITORIES
AROUND
1850 to 1854 ISH

N
W E
S

STATES

STATES

new territories should allow
slavery. President Pierce
tried to keep both sides
happy, but he made some poor decisions.
It didn't take long before many people felt
that Franklin Pierce wasn't a very good
president at all.

Franklin Pierce was born in a small, cramped, log cabin. His father, Benjamin, soon built a larger, more comfortable house for his family. Benjamin Pierce was a farmer, but he was also interested in public service. He was elected a city councilman and then became a sheriff. Years later, he was elected governor of New Hampshire.

   As a young man, Franklin's father had been
a commander in the Revolutionary War. He
had fought in the famous Battle of Bunker Hill.
Franklin and his brothers and sisters loved
hearing their father tell about his exciting war
adventures. Franklin's greatest dream was
to become a soldier someday.

As a young boy, Franklin Pierce went to school at the local schoolhouse. Later, he went away to boarding school. When it was time for college, he went off to Bowdoin College in the nearby state of Maine. While there, Franklin spent more time partying than studying. Then something happened that totally changed Franklin's attitude about school.

Bowdoin College in the early 1800s

During Franklin's third year at college, class rankings were displayed for everyone to see. Franklin's name was almost at the bottom of the list! He was embarrassed and angry with himself. He made up his mind to change things right away. Franklin began to study hard, and he never missed another class.

Franklin became interested in politics while in college. He knew that if he were going to run for public office someday, he would have to know as much as possible about the laws of the United States. After he graduated, Franklin studied law. He became a lawyer in 1827 at the age of twenty-three. Over the years, Franklin became an excellent lawyer. He was very handsome, had a great speaking voice, and

made his cases interesting. Eventually, people came from all over to see him argue cases. In the 1800s, watching court cases was a type of entertainment. Franklin Pierce was one of the court's biggest stars!

Franklin's father, Benjamin Pierce, served as governor of New Hampshire.

Franklin often took time off from his law business to run for government jobs. He got a lot of help from his father, who was well liked and had many close friends in the government. Franklin was elected to the New Hampshire legislature when he was twenty-five. A few years later, he was elected to the United States House of Representatives.

By the time he was thirty-three years old, Franklin had become a U.S. senator! Franklin now spent a lot of time in the nation's capital, Washington, D.C. He made lots of new friends there. Many of them were from the southern states. Even though Franklin was from the North, he agreed with the southern view that southerners had the right to own slaves.

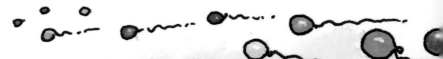

Before he became a senator, Franklin married Jane Appleton. Jane was the daughter of the former president of Bowdoin College. Franklin and Jane couldn't have been more different from each other. Jane was very shy and didn't like parties at all. She disliked people who drank alcohol, and she hated politics. It seemed as if Jane couldn't stand anything that Franklin enjoyed. It's amazing that they were attracted to each other.

An engraving of Jane Appleton Pierce

Franklin respected and loved his wife very much, though. In 1842, Franklin resigned from the Senate. He and Jane moved back to New Hampshire, where Franklin could spend more time with his family and take care of his law business.

Franklin promised Jane he would stay away from elections and government jobs. He even turned down an important job offered by his friend, President James Polk. Franklin kept busy, though, helping some of his friends get elected to government positions.

Then Franklin got a chance to make his lifelong dream come true. When the Mexican War began in 1846, Franklin joined the army to help serve his country. Franklin started out at the rank of private. Because of connections with friends in Washington, D.C., he was soon promoted to the rank of brigadier general!

A photograph of General Franklin Pierce taken during the Mexican War

Franklin was proud to help his country, but he also thought he could help his career if he became a war hero. Unfortunately, the war didn't go very well for Franklin. He was a general in charge of 2,500 men, but he had no military experience at all.

During the Battle of Churubusco (above), General Pierce injured his leg so badly that he fainted.

During one battle, General Pierce was thrown off his horse. He was seriously injured and passed out from the pain. In all the confusion, some soldiers thought Franklin was trying to get out of the fighting and called him a coward. This insult hurt Franklin Pierce more than any injury. When the war ended, a disappointed Franklin headed home to New Hampshire and re-opened his law business.

During Franklin Pierce's time, there were two main political groups in the United States. One was called the Democratic Party. The other was called the Whig Party. Franklin Pierce was a Democrat. He was always glad to help any Democrat who was running for an elected government job. But, in the mid-1800s, there was a major disagreement among the Democrats.

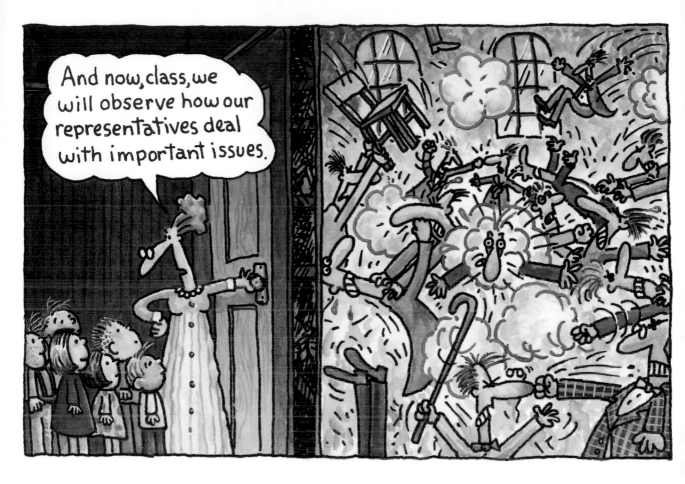

The U.S. Constitution gave people the right to own property. Some Democrats, including Franklin, believed this included human property—or slaves. Other Democrats didn't agree. They thought it was wrong for people to own slaves. The Whigs also argued among themselves about slavery. These conflicts led to lots of arguments in Congress. Some of them became violent.

A campaign poster for Franklin Pierce and his running mate William R. King

In 1852, when the Democratic Party was getting ready for the next presidential election, they had another big problem. Everyone was so angry with each other over what to do about slavery that they couldn't agree on whom their choice should be to run for president. They did agree that they would need someone who was pleasant, good-looking, fun to be around, and an excellent speaker. The Democrats decided that Franklin Pierce should be their man.

The official White House portrait of President Franklin Pierce, by George P.A. Healy

Franklin hadn't held an elected government job in ten years, so he didn't have many enemies. Most importantly, Democrats felt Franklin might be able to please voters in the North and the South, since he was a northerner who wasn't against slavery. The Democrats' plan worked. In 1852, Franklin agreed to run for president, and he won the election!

When Franklin began his new job, tensions were running high. The North and South continued arguing about what to do with the new territories that would become states someday. A senator from Illinois, Stephen A. Douglas, suggested that the Nebraska Territory be divided in half into Nebraska and Kansas.

Senator Douglas said that when these two territories became states, the people who lived in them could vote and decide for themselves if they wanted slavery or not. Stephen A. Douglas convinced President Pierce that this would be a fair way to do things. President Pierce agreed and signed Douglas's plan. It was called the Kansas-Nebraska Act.

The Sand Hills of Nebraska as they appear today

This illustration shows armed men entering Kansas to pressure people to vote for slavery.

Unfortunately, the Kansas-Nebraska Act caused more problems than President Pierce could ever have imagined. First of all, the act canceled out an agreement called The Missouri Compromise. This compromise had promised there would be no slavery in new territories north of a certain line. When the Missouri Compromise was done away with, it made abolitionists, or people against slavery, furious!

Right away, people from the South began sending hundreds of armed troublemakers into Kansas to convince settlers there to vote for slavery. Soon the abolitionists sent their own armed men to Kansas. In a few weeks, the territory became a lawless mess. Hundreds of people were killed or injured, and the territory became known as "Bleeding Kansas."

Terrible fighting broke out after the Kansas-Nebraska Act became law.

Bleeding Kansas took up most of President Pierce's time. People all over the country were beginning to think the president was wishy-washy and not doing enough to bring law and order to Kansas.

THE OLD SERVANT AND THE NEW.
Scene, "White House"—Time, 4th of March, 1857.

MRS. COLUMBIA.—Franklin, your time is out, and you may go back to your friends. Your recommendations wer good, but I am sorry to say you have not fulfilled my expectations. I hope James will do better, for I am nearly worried to death with these servan's.

This 1857 political cartoon shows President Pierce as a servant being sent away for having done a bad job. On the left is the "new servant," President-elect James Buchanan.

President Pierce didn't have much luck handling foreign problems, either. He did make one successful deal with Mexico, though. The United States bought about 30,000 square miles (77,700 square kilometers) of land from Mexico and finalized the Mexican-American border.

At the end of his term, Franklin Pierce didn't have many accomplishments to talk about. He did not serve a second four-year term. Franklin's own Democratic Party refused to nominate him as a candidate.

Franklin Pierce as an older man

Many historians think Franklin Pierce wasn't a very good president. By letting himself get pushed into signing the Kansas-Nebraska Act, he nudged the United States closer to civil war.

Franklin Pierce left his job as president in March of 1857. He and Jane traveled for two years in Europe, then headed back to their home in Concord, New Hampshire. Franklin Pierce died on October 8, 1869, four years after the Civil War ended.